Eva Hoffman

INTRODUCING CHILDREN TO THEIR AMAZING BRAINS

Illustrations by Justina Langley

LEARN TO LEARN

ISBN - 0 9535387 53
       - 9780953538751

Published by LEARN TO LEARN

LTL Books Ltd.
Court Lodge
Castlethorpe
Brigg, Nth. Lincs.
DN20 9LG - UK
Tel +44 (0)1652 650352
Fax +44 (0)1652 650372
www.ltlbooks.co.uk
info@ltlbooks.co.uk

Other titles by Dr Eva Hoffman:

'The Learning Adventure'   - ISBN 0953538702
'A Guide to The Learning Adventure'   - ISBN 0953538710
'For You, Dear Teacher'   - ISBN 0953538788
'Mind Mapping in Primary Classrooms'   - ISBN 0953538796
'Polish Children in English Schools'   - ISBN 0953538761

'Introducing Children To...'   (series of 4 titles) - Series ISBN 095353877X

                    ... Mind Mapping'   - ISBN 0953538745
                    ... Their Intelligences'   - ISBN 0953538729
                    ... Their Senses'   - ISBN 0953538737
                    ... Their Amazing Brains'   - ISBN 0953538753

Printed in England

INTRODUCING CHILDREN TO THEIR AMAZING BRAINS

DOESN'T IT SOMETIMES AMAZE YOU HOW VERY DIFFERENT PEOPLE ARE?

Think for a moment about your family members... your friends and their friends... people you work with… the children you teach.... Could you possibly find two people with identical likes and dislikes, who always think identical thoughts, who have identical attitudes, feelings, understanding, values, tastes, preferences? Very unlikely.
No two people on this planet are exactly the same, no two brains are identical.

Brain research brings a constant flow of new information, which is as fascinating as it can be confusing. This unbelievably complex organ every one of us has between our ears remains vastly a mystery. We are not born with a little book of instructions telling us how to use our brain. This little omission, however, shouldn't stop us from making the best use of what we *DO* know.
Discovering your own brain wiring is one of the most fascinating adventures you can experience; discovering how other people's brains work has the potential to lead to better understanding, tolerance and acceptance of others.

There are three things I would like to bring to your attention before you embark on this journey of discovery with children.

The first is the question of **HEMISPHERIC DOMINANCE**.
Our 'thinking brain', the Cortex, is divided into two halves, called Logic (Left) and Gestalt (Right) hemispheres. The left is also called the 'academic' brain and the right is often called the 'creative, artistic' brain. The two hemispheres are connected by a bundle of nerve cells which make it possible for information to travel from one hemisphere to the other. A simplified version of research findings suggests that each hemisphere is responsible for different functions. You have probably come across people talking about themselves or others in terms of their right or left 'brain'. It is true that there is a certain amount of specialization on the left and right side of the neo-cortex and that this specialization influences the way we respond to the world around us. However, we now know that every complex task involves BOTH sides of the brain and that it is not at all certain that one or the other hemisphere 'switches on' when we perform a specific task. Researches investigating hemispheric dominance have turned to looking at the degree to which one side of the brain is dominant, not at the absolute dominance of one over the other.
Although the question of dominance is under investigation, there can be little doubt that most of us have a tendency to think, feel and act in certain ways, which may also be attributed to our brain dominance. It is usually easier to notice it when we are under stress and have least control - that's when our 'masteral' tendencies are most obvious.

Learning new things puts the brain/body system under stress. This is why it is useful to know which hemispheric dominance we get locked in under stress, and what we can do about it.

The second thing I want to draw your attention to is the question of **BRAIN INTEGRATION**.
The brain is able to function well and learn easily when the internal and external conditions are making full integration possible. You are in a fully integrated state

- when there is access to all functions of the thinking brain (Gestalt and Logic),
- when there is an easy flow of information because all parts of the brain are communicating with each other,
- when there are no blockages in the subconscious processing centres.

This, however, is an ideal state, enjoyed by very few people, less than two percent of the world population, according to Charles Krebs. So what about the rest of us? Are we doomed or is there anything we can do about it?

A vast majority of us are learning blocked; the interesting thing is that even those of us who have been fairly successful at school as well as in life also have blockages which, when removed, result in better learning.
Easy and enjoyable learning can be achieved through finding out how your brain functions and how to improve its integration. There are courses that teach you how you can do it as well as books showing some very useful self-help techniques (see bibliography).

Finally, I want to invite you to consider the crucial, and yet frequently forgotten, **NON-CONSCIOUS mind**.
We are very much aware of the importance of our conscious mind; we know it is responsible for deliberate thinking, for analysis and problem solving, for reasoning, justification and evaluating ideas. However, we don't often remember that it is the non-conscious mind which deals with processing everything that the conscious mind provides it with. It is the non-conscious mind that constantly generates ideas. This is the mind associated with wisdom and creativity, which is holistic and which asks questions rather than answers them.
So when you see a child daydreaming, gazing out of the window, just 'being', bear in mind that he or she may be processing information or creating new ideas.

Daydreaming was Einstein's favourite pastime!

The activities in this book are designed to take each child on her or his own brain discovery adventure, so that they may understand themselves better and become aware of what exactly they need to improve their thinking and learning. What we want to avoid is putting labels on children. This is not only unnecessary but can be seriously harmful.

Whatever children discover about their brains, they need to be reminded that:

- this is what their brains are like NOW
- their brains are constantly changing
- they have the power to positively influence their brain development
- there are ways which can make their brains work better
- in the meantime, they need to celebrate the incredibly brilliant and powerful brain each of them has!

By celebrating the brain we have, by focusing on our strengths, on what we *CAN* do rather than on what we cannot, by appreciating that our brain wiring has the potential to change and that there are things we can do to make this happen, we may be able to achieve more than we have ever imagined.

This is the message I would like all children to get.

I would also like them to gain an understanding of themselves and, very importantly, of others. This is not only about learning better. I hope this understanding will lead to more patience, more tolerance, more acceptance. It will enable them to enjoy and celebrate the wonderful diversity of people on this planet of ours.

This is my dream and the dream of many others I know. We believe it will come true one day.

Eva Hoffman

Activity 1a

Teacher's notes

The purpose of this first activity is simply raising children's awareness, leading to better understanding, accepting, appreciating and celebrating the differences between people.

Treat this activity as a game. If possible, invite other adults to participate in it, too.

At this stage it is not necessary to explain anything other than to **encourage children to notice how different other people's responses are from their own**.

This first activity is presented in two different 'user friendly' forms for those who prefer either linear or radiant notes.

Tell the children that all the activities are part of an exciting and enjoyable exploration of our wonderfully diverse minds.

Remind the children that it is neither good nor bad to be the way they are.

- EVERYBODY IS DIFFERENT
- PEOPLE LIKE DIFFERENT THINGS

Find a person who:

1. forgets things when she/he is nervous

2. likes to be challenged to solve a problem

3. has pictures in his or her head, likes day dreaming

4. likes to put things neatly in order

5. enjoys word games, writing or reading

6. loves music, rhythm, singing / playing an instrument

7. notices small things even when nervous

8. feels that colours are important, likes colourful things

9. reads the end of the book first before reading the rest

10. likes black and white pictures more than colour paintings

11. likes cosy rooms and cuddly things

12. can solve problems and answer questions even when nervous

1a

and write their name in the box.

Activity 1b

Teacher's notes

The purpose of this first activity is simply raising children's awareness, leading to better understanding, accepting, appreciating and celebrating the differences between people.

Treat this activity as a game. If possible, invite other adults to participate in it, too.

At this stage it is not necessary to explain anything other than to **encourage children to notice how different other people's responses are from their own.**

This first activity is presented in two different 'user friendly' forms for those who prefer either linear or radiant notes.

Tell the children that all the activities are part of an exciting and enjoyable exploration of our wonderfully diverse minds.

Remind the children that it is neither good nor bad to be the way they are.

- EVERYBODY IS DIFFERENT
- PEOPLE LIKE DIFFERENT THINGS

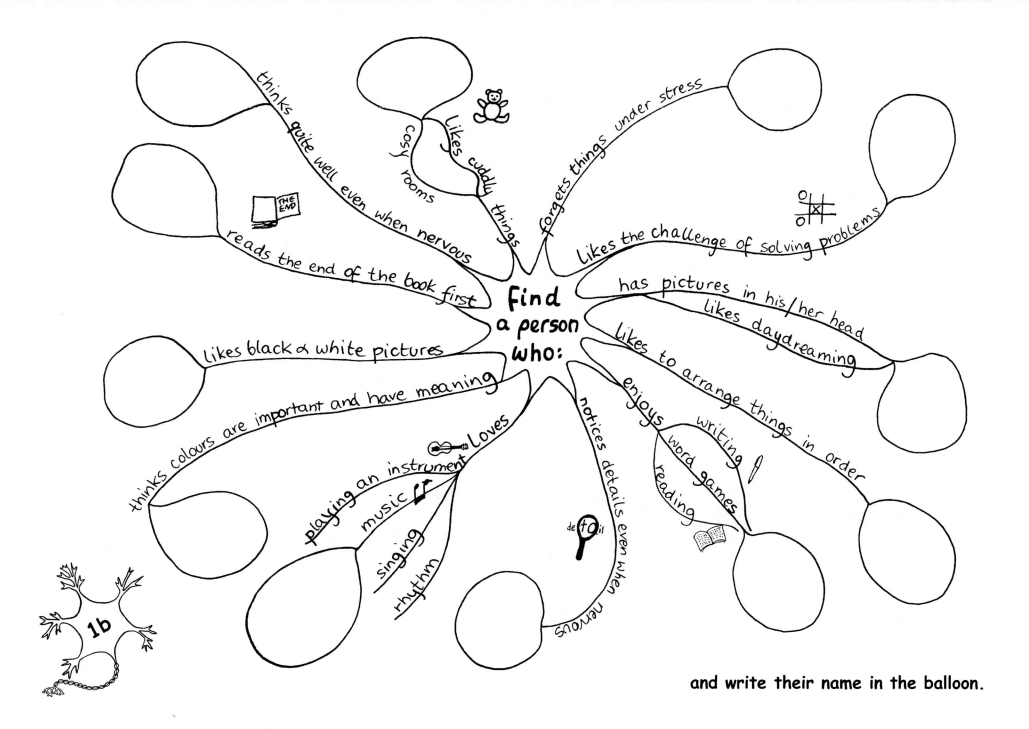

Find a person who:

- thinks quite well even when nervous
- Likes cosy rooms
- Likes cuddly things
- forgets things under stress
- Likes the challenge of solving problems
- reads the end of the book first
- has pictures in his/her head
- likes daydreaming
- likes black & white pictures
- likes to arrange things in order
- thinks colours are important and have meaning
- Loves playing an instrument / music / singing / rhythm
- notices details even when nervous
- enjoys writing / word games / reading

1b

and write their name in the balloon.

When you have played the game (Activity 1), tell the children you will introduce them to something wonderful and absolutely amazing, something they have had ever since they were born and yet don't know very much about... to their unique brains!

Teacher's notes

Ask children why it may be a very good idea to understand how their brains work.

What comes with every new electronic toy you get, with every electronic appliance such as a VCR...?
Yes, a book of instructions.
What do we need the books of instructions for...?
Instructions tell you how your toy works, how it is made inside and how to put it together. The instructions may also tell you how to take care of your toy so that it may work well for a long time and what to do when something goes wrong.

The brain is the most amazing, most complex, and most wonderful thing ever created. What is more, it is absolutely unique, different from the brain of anybody else in the whole wide world! It is infinitely more complex than any toy you will ever get and yet, when you were born you didn't pop out of your mother's womb with a little book of instructions telling you how to use your incredibly complex brain, did you?

THE TRIUNE BRAIN

- The **Reptilian Brain** - it is our survival brain responsible for our physiological functions: heart rate, breathing, temperature and digestion. Programmed to protect, it controls our instinctive responses.
- The **Mammalian Brain,** also called the **Limbic Brain** - it is considered to be the centre of our emotions. The focus of its non-conscious operations is survival. It controls our instincts and basic drives like eating, drinking and sexuality.
- The **Cortex** (the Thinking Brain) is uniquely human - this logically thinking, problem solving, rationally reasoning, abundantly creative brain has six layers, each playing a different role. It controls the emotional Limbic Brain.

Ask the children whether they would prefer to read the story themselves or to hear you read it to them. If possible, give the text to the ones who want to read it for themselves and read the story to the remaining group.

Ask the children what they remember from the story about their brains. Discuss their answers with them. Then ask them to fill their Activity 2 sheets.

These may be new and difficult words but many children we worked with were fascinated with the brain terminology and showed great interest in mastering it.

Encourage children to share with the others what they have learned.

Later, to reinforce the learning, you may want to divide the class into groups of four and have children act out the 'Brain Story' as if it was a play.

THE BRAIN STORY

In the middle of the night Nikki was suddenly woken up by yelling, screaming and shouting, not a pleasant way to wake up from your dreams!
For a while she was too sleepy to be able to tell what was happening; she sat up in bed and started listening to the argument, which she now realized was clearly going on in her head...

- *'I am the most important brain here!'* screamed the Reptilian Brain. *'Without me Nikki wouldn't be alive!'*

- *'What's the good of being alive if you don't even KNOW that you're alive! You don't know what you're doing, you can't even think!'* yelled the Cortex.

- *'Ha, I certainly know what I'm doing! I am in control here! I am responsible for her safety! I warn her about any danger she may be in! I am responsible for her quick reactions so that she can protect herself from harm! When she puts her finger in the fire, I'm the one who takes it away in a fraction of a second!'* shouted the Reptilian Brain.

- *'Oh, don't try to be so clever, every animal has a Reptilian Brain!'* snubbed the Cortex. *'Anything else you can do?'*

- *'Sure! I take care of her breathing, heart rate, her digestion and her body temperature. Can you get any more important than that?'* replied the Reptilian Brain.

- *'Oh, well, so you may be important... a little'*, said the Cortex, who was beginning to see some sense in the Reptilian Brain's words. *'However, Nikki is a human because she has me!'*

- *'Oh yeah, and why is this?'* sneered the Reptilian Brain, feeling less sure of himself.

- *'I am responsible for Nikki's ability to think. Because of me she can* understand the world around her, because of me she can count, read, and use her computer. Nikki's life would make no sense without me because she wouldn't be a human!' exclaimed the Cortex.

There was a long silence… Nikki started thinking about going back to sleep when she heard a soft, gentle voice:

- 'You've forgotten about me. I'm just as important as you two.'

'I wonder who this can be?' thought Nikki. 'Who are you?', she asked.

- 'I am your Limbic Brain. Because of me you can feel joy and sadness, anxiety and love. What would your life be worth without your feelings? All the thinking in the world cannot bring you love and caring.'

- 'Well, yes…', uttered the Cortex, '…I suppose you're right, feelings are important. Anything else you do?'

- 'I am Nikki's memory', the Limbic Brain turned to the Cortex. 'Without me she wouldn't be able to learn and remember things. I control her sleep, her hunger and thirst. I also protect Nikki from getting ill. Is that not enough?'

Both the Cortex and the Reptilian Brain were listening carefully to what the Limbic Brain was saying. Both were thinking of a reply.
Nikki knew that the only way she could get some sleep was to quickly resolve the conflict:
- 'I understand I couldn't live without you, my dear Reptilian Brain. My life would not be possible without you, my sweet Limbic Brain; and I certainly couldn't be without you, my precious Cortex. Without you, my Cortex, I wouldn't really KNOW that I am alive, I wouldn't be able to understand and experience the world around me. Without you I wouldn't be able to think about… thinking!'

- 'Are you saying that all of us are equally important?' quietly asked the Cortex.

- 'I certainly am', answered Nikki. 'Besides, you are not really three separate brains. In fact the three of you together make this ONE Amazing Brain that I am privileged to have. Thank you all very, very much!...
And now, if you'll excuse me, I would really like to get some sleep! Goodnight.'

Just imagine - you have three brains in one! Below, the simplified cross-section of the Triune Brain (three-in-one) shows how our brains evolved over four billion (!) years. All animals have the Reptilian Brain; mammals have the Reptilian and the Mammalian (Limbic) Brain; only humans have the Cortex (the 'Thinking Brain') on top of the other two.

In the clouds write three things you remember about each part of the brain.

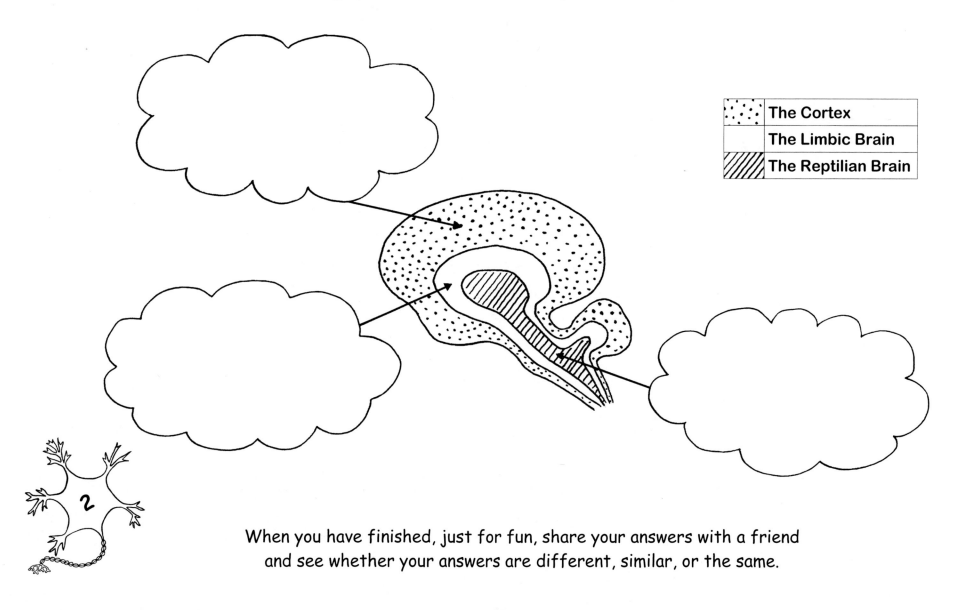

∴∵∴	The Cortex
	The Limbic Brain
⫻	The Reptilian Brain

When you have finished, just for fun, share your answers with a friend and see whether your answers are different, similar, or the same.

Activity 3

Teacher's notes

BRAIN QUESTIONS

In the following section of the book there are some questions and answers about the brain.

Photocopy the Question pages on, say, yellow sheets and the Answer pages on a different colour paper.

Laminate each separate question together with its corresponding answer on the back.

Put children in groups of three or four and give each group **a selection** of questions depending on their age and the level of interest. Then ask each child to find the most interesting question, something they would like to know.

Only when every child has found an interesting question let them turn over the sheets and read the answers.

Let each of them tell somebody else what they have learned.

At the end of each session ask them to write or draw three interesting things about the brain (Activity 3 sheets).

This activity may be repeated several times, in-between the other activities in the book, as long as children find the Q's & A's sessions interesting.

Beware of making the sessions too long! If you give them too much at once, the fun is gone.

Encourage children to share with someone what they have learned.

Write the three most interesting things you have learned about your brain today.

When you have finished, just for fun, share your answers with a friend
and see whether your answers are different, similar, or the same.

What are neurons?

What do neurons do?

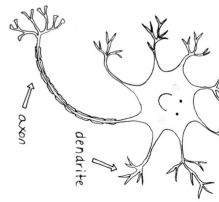

A neuron consists of:

- a cell body,
- many *dendrites* - branch-like extensions that grow outward from the cell body,
- one *axon* - a leg-like extension, 1 - 100 cm long, that connects with dendrites of other neurons.

Each brain cell can grow 20,000 'branches' to connect with other cells' branches.

Every axon splits itself to connect with dendrites of thousands of other cells.

You have around 100 billion neurons in your brain, your heart and throughout your body's nervous system.

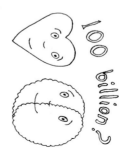

A.1

Neurons communicate with each other producing thoughts, feelings and actions.

Information flows from the cell body down the *axon*.

Information is carried down the axon by electrical impulses.

Axon tips are filled with chemicals called *neurotransmitters*.

A gap between an *axon* of one cell and a *dendrite* of another is called a *synaptic gap* or a *synapse*.

Information is transmitted across the synaptic gap between neurons when *neurotransmitters* are released by electrical stimulations.

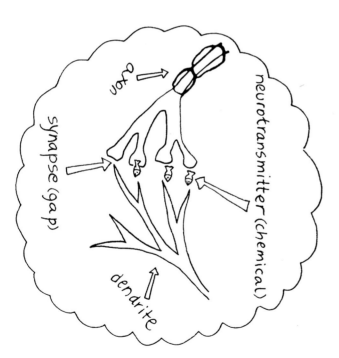

neurotransmitter (chemical)

axon

synapse (gap)

dendrite

A.2

How do the brain chemicals get into my brain?

Are my parents responsible for the brain I have?

YOU MAKE THEM YOURSELF!

Your brain makes
- painkillers,
- calming chemicals,
- 'happy' chemicals,
- energizing chemicals.

When you move some of your muscles,
you produce *dopamine* - a pleasure chemical and a painkiller;
when you relax,
you produce *serotonin* - a calming chemical;
when you smile or laugh,
you produce *endorphin* - a 'happy' chemical;
when you run or move a lot,
you produce *adrenaline* - an energizing chemical;
when you are stressed,
you produce **a lot of** adrenaline which switches off your thinking.
(A little of adrenaline may be good for your brain but too much may be harmful.)

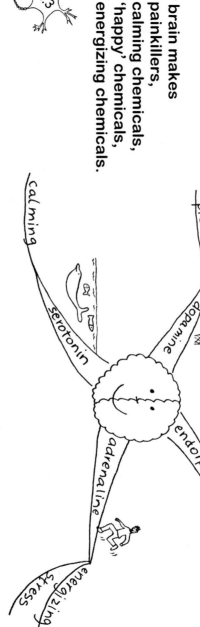

YOU CAN MAKE YOUR BRAIN SMARTER. IT IS UP TO YOU!

In fact, YOU are responsible for your brain much more than your parents.

YOU can change your brain structure, create new connections and get rid of others.

Learn as many new and different things as you can!

Think positive thoughts which are helpful and good for your well-being, like: *'I can do whatever I decide to do, if I put my mind to it and do my best'.*

When you learn new things and *when you expect to do well*, your brain will grow, creating new connections between the cells.

What happens in my brain when I learn something new?

How do my brain cells communicate with each other?

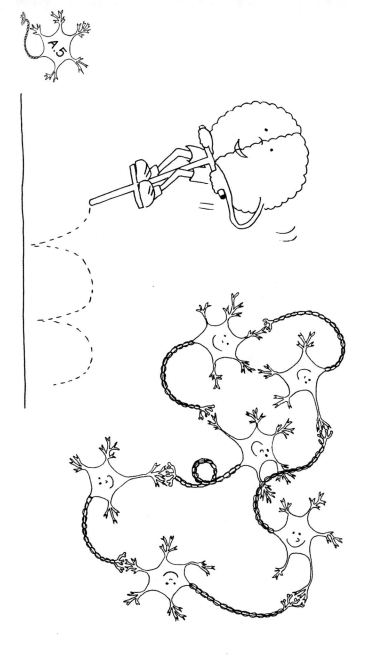

Every time you learn something, and not only at school, your brain cells connect to more brain cells and create new patterns.

This way your brain develops and you get smarter.

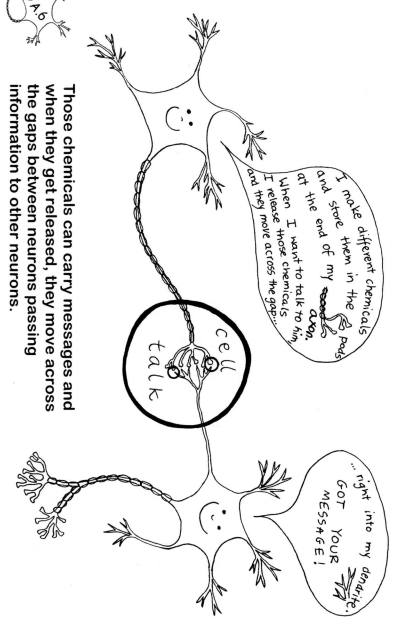

Different chemicals, called *neurotransmitters*, created inside neurons are stored in small pods (*vesicles*) at the end of every *axon*.

Those chemicals can carry messages and when they get released, they move across the gaps between neurons passing information to other neurons.

Is my brain the same now as it was when I was born?

How do I create a thought in my brain?

A.7

Your brain structure changes every time you experience something and learn something new.

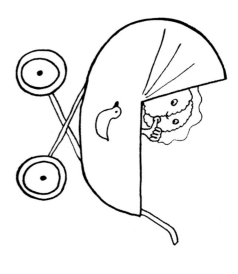

It also changes every time you think a thought.

That is why it is very important to think good thoughts.

It is good to think or say *'I can do it when I do my best'* and definitely not good to think or say

'I can never do anything right'.

A.8

There is a gap between an *axon* of one neuron (a nerve cell) and a *dendrite* of another neuron.

This gap is called a *synaptic gap* or a *synapse*.

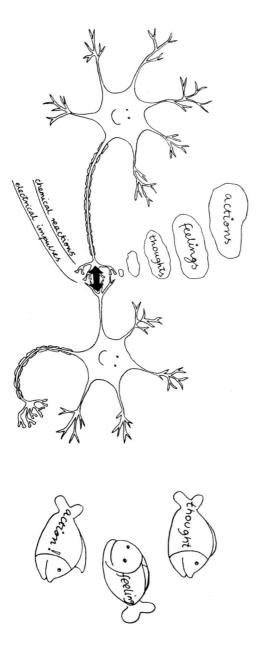

A thought is created in your brain when *neurotransmitters*, chemicals produced in the brain, flow across the gap between *axons* and *dendrites*.

Your feelings and your behaviours are created the same way.

When does my brain learn better:
when I ask questions or when I answer questions?

Which part of my brain is the first
to get information?

When you are curious to know something, you brain is ready to learn.

Your brain learns really well when you think of questions about the topic you are learning.

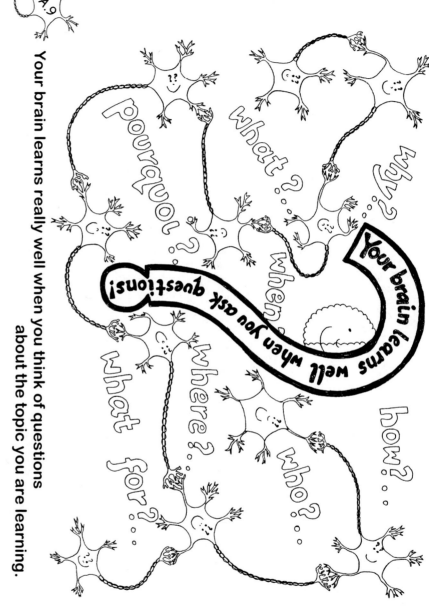

The *hippocampus*, a small sea-horse-shaped part of your limbic brain gets information from your senses, i.e. seeing, hearing, smell, touch and taste.

You will remember information best when you connect it with some events, time and place; linking it to something that happened in real life.

For example

- making calculations in a shop,
- learning about animals in the zoo or on a farm.

Can you think of other examples?

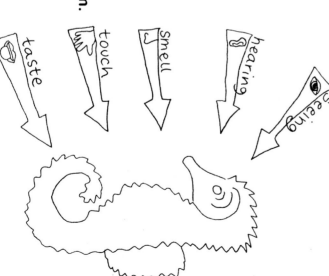

Does learning happen only in the brain?

Q.11

Why is movement good for learning?

Q.12

When you move your arms, legs or feet to the other side of your body (across the body's vertical mid-line) you send impulses to the nerves connecting both sides (hemispheres) of the brain.

This makes your whole brain work together.
Much better than doing the work with one half only!

In fact, over 90% of you brain cells' communication, which is very important part of learning, takes place somewhere else in your body.

98% OF NEURONE COMMUNICATION HAPPENS IN YOUR BODY

Your body/brain *neurons* become active when you move.

WHEN YOU MOVE YOU MAKE YOUR NEURONES ACTIVE!

Before you sit down to do your homework it is good to spin, swing, run, then stop and slowly breathe in... and out... in... and out...

Which hemisphere is better: right or left?

How does my brain work: in lines or in all directions?

Your brain works best when there is good communication between the two hemispheres.

When you are under stress, your right and left hemispheres may have difficulties communicating with each other.

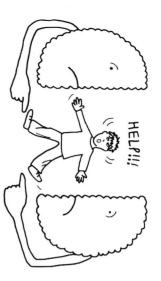

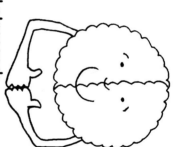

Here is what you can do when you feel stressed:

- take a deep breath... and another one,
- give yourself 'a pat on the back'
  - pat your *left shoulder* with your *right hand* and your *right thigh* with your *left hand*, then your *right shoulder* with your *left hand* and your *left thigh* with your *right hand*;
- cross your arms and legs and take three deep breaths... (*TRY IT, IT WORKS!*)

Your brain works best when you're reading or writing in lines, your brain works in lines too.

Your brain works both in lines and in a radiant way.

When you're reading or writing in lines, your brain works in lines too.

Thinking in a radiant way and using radiant notes helps many people come up with new ideas, organize their thoughts and remember better.

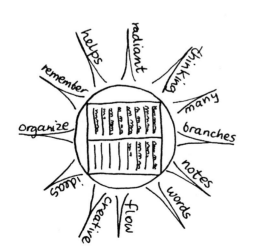

TO HELP YOUR BRAIN WORK IN A RADIANT WAY, LEARN TO USE MIND MAPPING.

Why does my brain often want to have a rest?

Q.15

Why do I have to learn the same thing over and over again?

Q.16

Your brain must pay attention when you are learning something; however, to really understand things many of us need some quiet time for the brain to make sense of the learning.

Some scientists say that your brain can either pay attention or make sense of the learning – it cannot do these two things at the same time.

Give your hard working brain a break every 8–10 minutes (!):

- have a drink of water,
- take a few deep breaths,
- move a little,
- then get back to your work.

When you repeat something, the connections between neurons become stronger and this helps you remember better.

Repetition helps to insulate *axons* with a substance called *myelin*, which forms around well-used axons.

The thicker the axon the better it works and there is better communication between the cells.

The right kind of food, such as

- oily fish,
- soybean,
- olive and sunflower oil,

also helps to insulate your axons.

How can I remember things better?

Q.17

Does my brain really need fresh air?

Q.18

A.17

MIND MAPPING · TALKING THROUGH · ACTING OUT · COLOURS · UNDERSTANDING · REAL LIFE LINK · CHANGE PICTURES · CHANGE · BREAKS · MOVEMENT · OXYGEN · RIGHT FOOD · WATER · HOW CAN I REMEMBER THINGS BETTER?

- Give your brain the right kind of food such as fish, vegetables, fruits and nuts.
- Drink plenty of water.
- Open windows to get plenty of oxygen.
- Move before and possibly while you are learning (swing your legs, doodle, chew gum, play with BLU Tack).
- Give your brain frequent breaks.
- Change what you are learning as often as you need (at home!).
- Create in your mind pictures of what you are learning.
- Attach what you are learning to some real-life situation.
- Try to understand *why* you are learning this (ask your teacher); one of the reasons may simply be helping your brain develop!
- Use colours for highlighting and drawing pictures.
- Act out what you are learning; 'muscle-based' memory created through touch and movement builds longer lasting connections.
- Talk to someone about the thing you are learning or teach it to somebody else.
- Use mind mapping

Air may be charged negatively (-) or positively (+).

Your brain likes negatively (-) charged fresh air (especially after the rain, a shower or near waterfalls).

The negatively (-) charged air has a *positive* effect.
It helps the brain produce good chemicals.
These chemicals relax the brain and help it grow.

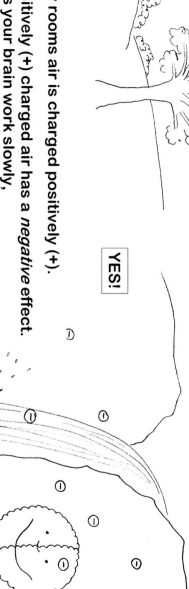

YES!

A.18

In stuffy rooms air is charged positively (+).

The positively (+) charged air has a *negative* effect.
It makes your brain work slowly,
making you feel stressed and tired.

**REMEMBER
TO LET FRESH AIR INTO THE ROOM BEFORE YOU START YOUR WORK.**

Why do people say that my brain likes water?

Q.19

When is my brain most ready to learn?

Q.20

Your body/brain system runs on electrical and chemical reactions and those reactions need plenty of water!

When your brain and your body have no water, they work much more slowly and less effectively.

- When what you are learning surprises you.
- At the beginning of a lesson.
- At the end of a lesson.
- When you are learning about something new.
- When you are having fun.
- When learning gives you strong feelings.

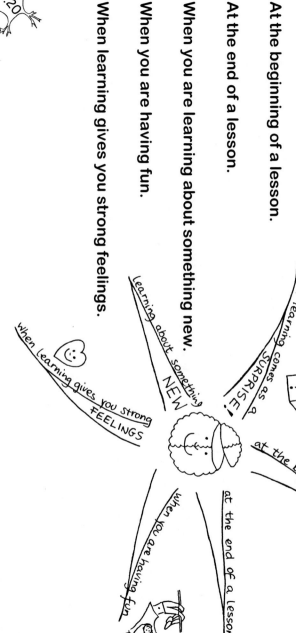

when learning comes as a SURPRISE!

learning about something NEW

when learning gives you strong FEELINGS

at the beginning of a lesson

at the end of a lesson

when you are having fun

What have my feelings to do with learning?

Q.21

What is it that my brain doesn't like?

Q.22

Your strong feelings are stored in the *amygdala*, the almond-shaped part of the limbic brain; the same part of the brain is also responsible for your memory.

When you learn with emotions, it is much easier to remember things.

Think of something exciting, wonderful, scary or really interesting that has happened to you....

Can you remember it really well?...
If you do, it is because your brain remembers well things which create strong feelings in you.

Think of happy things when you're learning.
Make the things you're learning your friends,
feel positive towards them.

When you feel bad about learning, your brain produces chemicals called *neuro-inhibitors* which make learning difficult or even impossible.

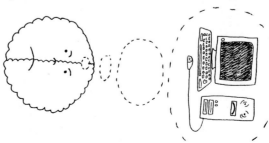

A.21

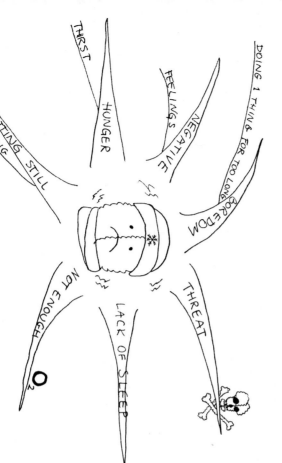

Your brain 'freezes' or switches off

- when you feel threatened or scared,
- when you feel bad about something you are doing,
- when you do the same thing for a very long time,
- when you sit in one position for a long time,
- when there is not enough oxygen in the room,
- when you don't get enough sleep,
- when you are thirsty or hungry.

THIRST

HUNGER

FEELINGS NEGATIVE

DOING 1 THING FOR TOO LONG BOREDOM

SITTING STILL FOR TOO LONG

NOT ENOUGH O_2

LACK OF SLEEP

THREAT

A.22

What can I do when I feel stressed or when my brain feels worried?

What has slouching to do with my brain?

When you are stressed, you cannot think or learn.
Your channels for learning are closed!

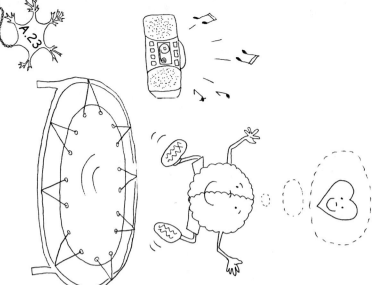

Your brain releases a chemical called *cortisol*, and too much cortisol can be harmful.

To control the cortisol:

- take a few deep breaths (first open the window!),
- make large muscle movements (this produces *dopamine*),
- smile this produces *endorphins*),
- exercise (this produces *adrenalin*),
- think about something pleasant,
- listen to music which makes you feel good.

A.23

When you slouch, the communication between neurons is difficult and you begin to feel low.

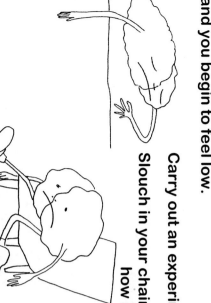

Carry out an experiment.

Slouch in your chair... frown a little... how are you feeling?

Straighten up, take a deep breath and smile... can you feel the difference?

When you sit or stand straight, you breathe freely and your energy flows freely, too.

Whenever you begin to slouch, notice it and change your body posture *from slump to pump!*

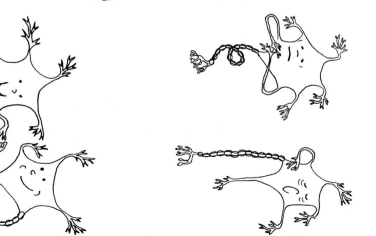

A.24

Why is it sometimes difficult for me to pay attention?

How long can my brain work without having a break?

A.25

- You may be thirsty - try drinking some water.
- You may be sleepy. What time did you go to bed last night?
- You may have too little oxygen - open the windows and let some fresh air in!
- You may be doing the same thing for too long - take a break or do something different.
- Maybe you don't move enough during the breaks - get up and stretch.
- You may have had too many sweet snacks - try fruit instead.
- You may have had too many fizzy drinks with artificial colouring, flavour or preservatives - back to the water

ALL THESE THINGS MAY AFFECT YOUR CONCENTRATION !

A.26

New connections in the brain need time to settle.
Your brain needs time to sort out the information it receives.
It does it naturally, by itself, if you give it a break every 8 - 15 minutes.

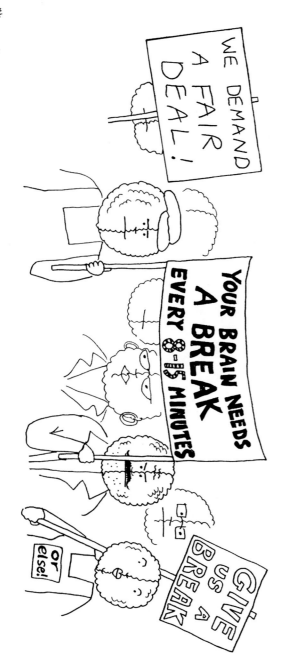

WE DEMAND A FAIR DEAL!

YOUR BRAIN NEEDS A BREAK EVERY 8-15 MINUTES

GIVE US A BREAK or else!

If you don't give it a break,
it will take time out by itself and you soon be daydreaming!

Does it really matter for the brain what I eat?

Q.27

What does my brain like?

Q.28

DO

Drink plenty of still water.
Eat oily fish (e.g. cod, tuna),
soybeans, peanuts
(if you are not allergic to them),
plenty of fresh vegetables
and fresh or dried fruit.

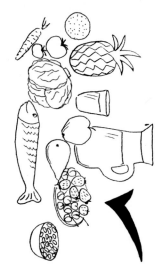

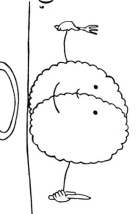

YES !!!
What you eat and what you drink makes a huge difference to how well your brain works.

AVOID

Avoid sweetened foods;
they send your energy
up for a while but then
soon you lose all that
energy and feel tired
and apathetic.
Avoid fizzy drinks
with artificial flavours
and colourings.
Natural fruit juices
are good because the
brain treats them as
food, not as drinks!

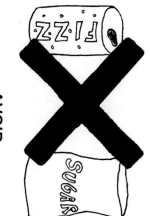

A.27

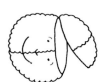

Your brain likes:

- 8 – 10 hours of sleep each day,
- fruit, vegetables and fish oil,
- a lot of fresh air (oxygen),
- a change of activities,
- to be stimulated,
- plenty of water.

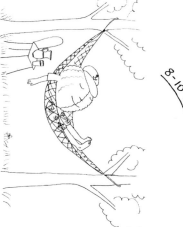

The brain does a lot of 'sorting out' when you are asleep.

A.28

Does my brain like pictures?

Q.29

Why does my brain sometimes seem to be 'switched off'?

Q.30

A.29

Out of an amazing 30 million bits of information taken by the eyes every second, the human brain can register over 36 thousand images per hour!

Isn't that amazing!

If YOU like pictures, to help your brain remember things:

* make pictures in your head of what you're learning;
* draw pictures of what you're learning;
* make charts, graphs and diagrams;
* use mind mapping;
* doodle while you listen;
* use colour when making notes, use highlighters;
* display your notes where you can see them.

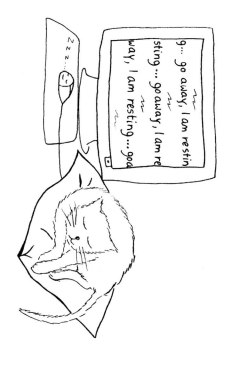

A.30

Like a computer screen saver, our thinking brain (*the cortex*) slides into a passive mode to save energy.

This happens when you are tired, bored, or when your brain has not enough oxygen.

You can 'turn the brain on' again by moving you body and breathing deeply,

actively looking, listening, touching,

tasting or smelling something,

doing something different

or doing the same thing in a different way.

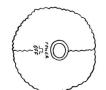

What grabs my brain's attention?

What has my heart to do with learning?

All these will certainly help you pay attention:

- something funny;
- something new;
- something different;
- something about YOU;
- and something that speaks to your heart.

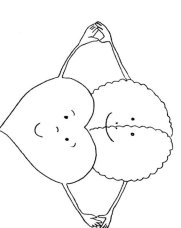

something about me? ...

The brain – heart connection is extremely important.

For a long time, until about 500 years ago, people thought that the 'thinking' organ was not in our head but in the heart ('learning by heart').

Now, we know it is not exactly so, but we also know that our feelings and emotions play very important part in our learning.

When we memorise things, it is much easier to remember them when our 'heart is in it'.

If your brain and your heart vibrate in harmony, you think better!

To help your brain and heart vibrate in harmony:

- smile often;
- think pleasant thoughts
  (appreciation, love, caring, hope);
- play music which makes you feel positive and relaxed;
- decide to have a positive attitude to your school, other people, your family, life in general;
- breathe deeply;
- relax your brain by gazing at trees or clouds, or by just sitting quietly.

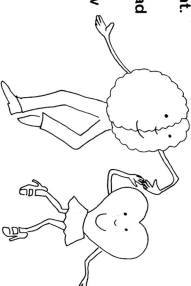

Is laughter good for learning?

Q.33

Can words harm the brain?

Q.34

Laughter helps you remember things

When you laugh, the brain's chemicals, which you need for paying attention and to remember things, flow freely.

When you laugh, your stress level goes down, and this is good for the brain and for learning.

YEE...HE...HE...SS!!!

BEST BRAIN JOKES

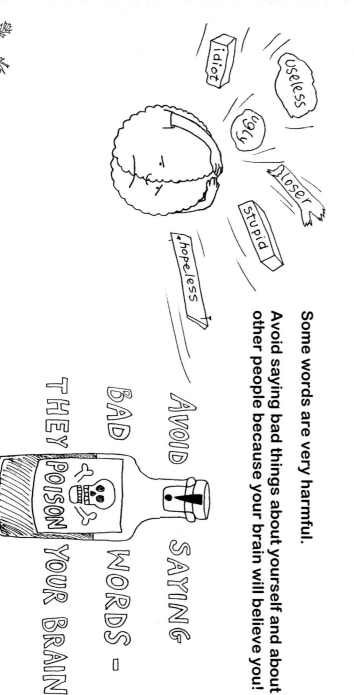

idiot · useless · ugly · loser · stupid · hopeless

Words influence your nervous system, your feelings and your actions.

Some words are very harmful.

Avoid saying bad things about yourself and about other people because your brain will believe you!

AVOID SAYING BAD WORDS – THEY POISON YOUR BRAIN

BAD WORDS AND BAD THOUGHTS POISON YOUR BRAIN AND YOUR HEART!

Can setting goals make my brain work better?

Q.35

Is it necessary to always be successful and never make mistakes?

Q.36

Thoughts about reaching the goal are pleasant for your brain

Thoughts about achieving what you want to achieve produce 'feel good' chemicals, called *endorphins*. They make you feel good and work with enthusiasm.

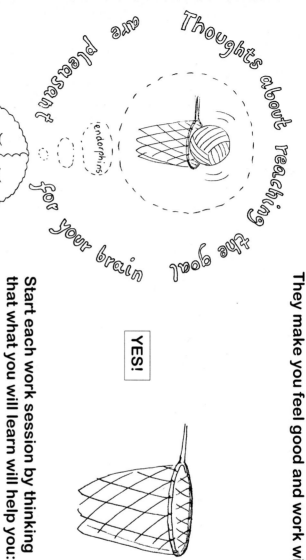

YES!

Start each work session by thinking that what you will learn will help you:

- be smarter,
- get good grades,
- feel good about yourself.

ABSOLUTELY NOT!

You can learn much more from your mistakes than from getting it right.

In fact, when you get it right the first time, you are not really *learning*.

O O P S ! . . . .

YOU CAN LEARN FROM MISTAKES!

Next time you make a mistake, say to yourself:
'GREAT! NOW I CAN REALLY LEARN THIS!'

Activity 4

Ask the children to tell you what **they think** the brain needs to work well.

Accept all answers but write on the board only the correct ones, then ask children to do Activity 4.

When they complete their notes, to reinforce what they have learned and as a reminder you may also want to give them a copy of this drawing to colour in.

Teacher's notes

the brain likes

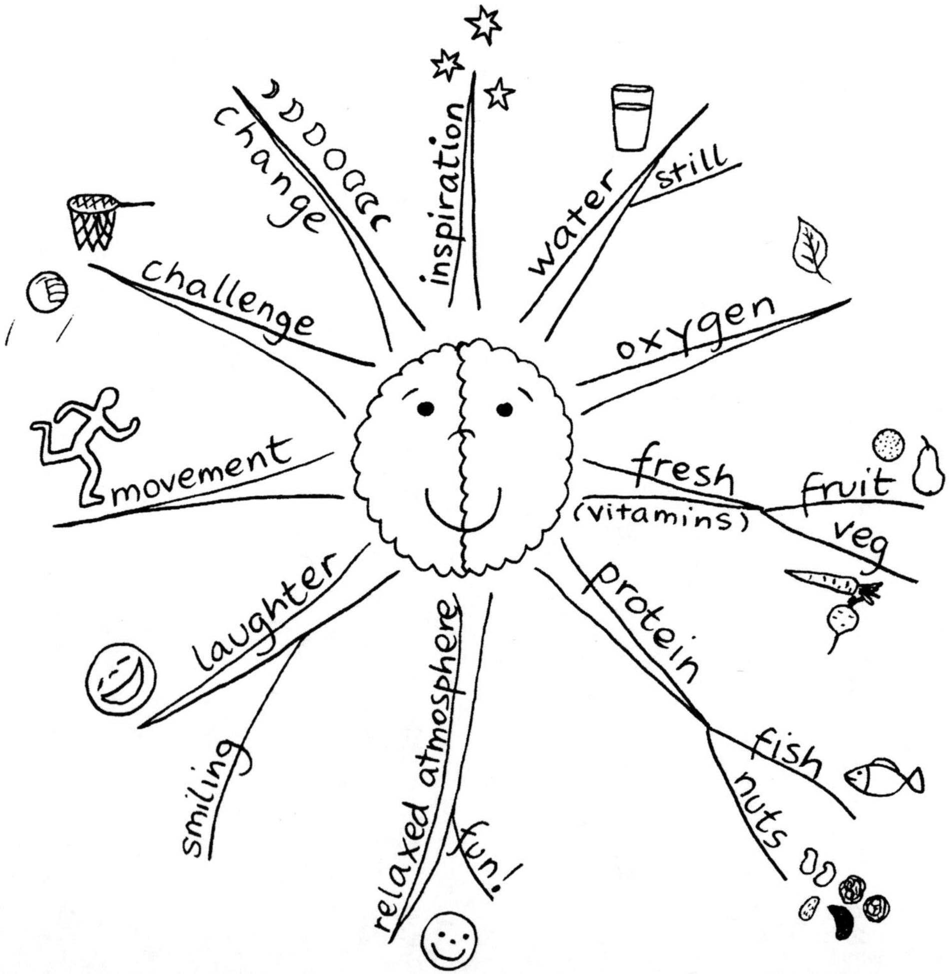

change
inspiration
water
still
challenge
oxygen
movement
fresh (vitamins)
fruit
veg
laughter
protein
smiling
relaxed atmosphere
fun!
fish
nuts

the brain doesn't like

frustration
irritation
anger
stuffy rooms
smoking!
caffeine
tension
stress
fizzy drinks
monotony
too much animal fat
LARD
SUGAR LUMPS
sitting still for too long
boredom
too much sugar

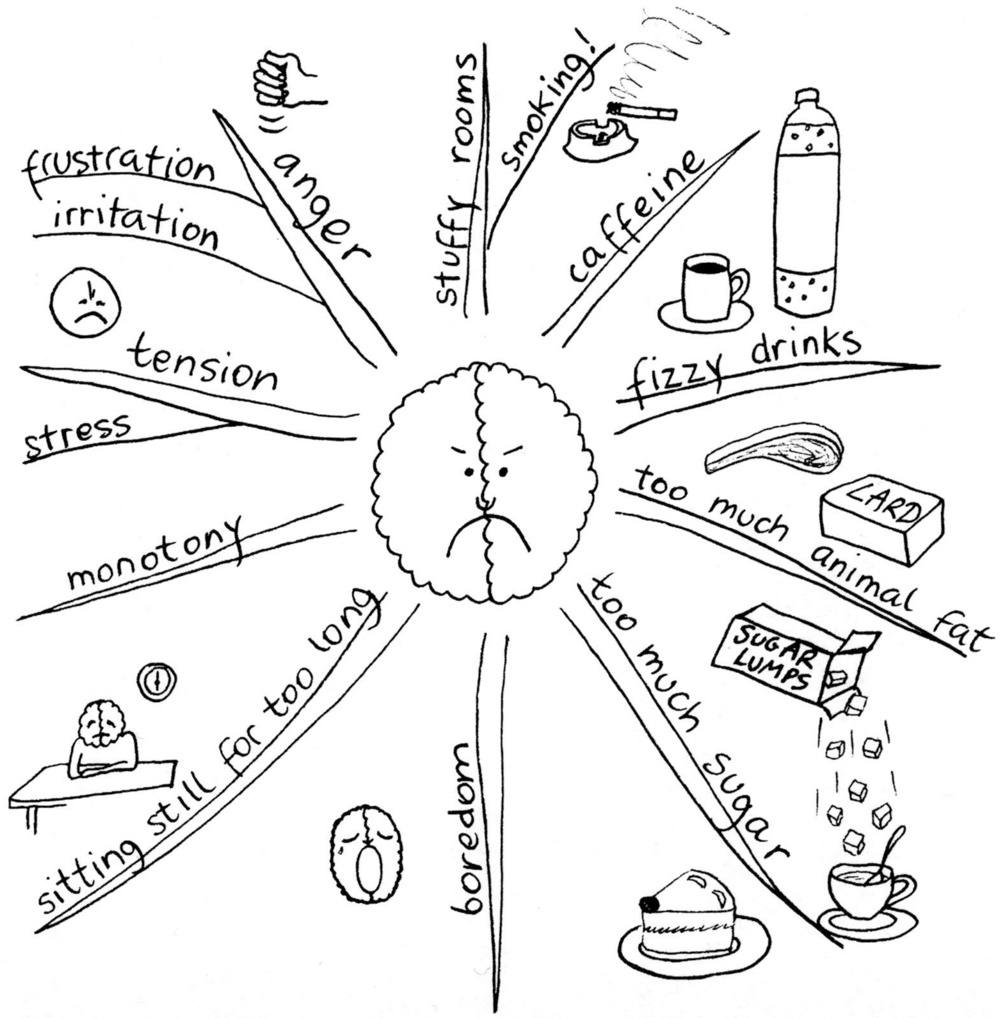

Around the picture of a happy brain write and draw everything the brain likes and needs to work well.
Around the picture of a miserable looking brain write and draw what is bad for the brain.
If you prefer working with a friend, you are welcome to do so.

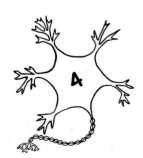

WHAT HAVE YOU LEARNED ABOUT YOUR BRAIN TODAY? Talk to your friend about it.

Activity 5

Teacher's notes

Ask the children to remember a situation when their **brain refused to work well** and ask them to think **why.** (Please emphasize that this does NOT have to be their school experience.)

Ask the children to remember a time when their **brain worked well** and ask them to think **why** in their opinion it worked well on that occasion.

Encourage them to look at Activity 4 in search for the answers. One of the purposes of this discovery process is to help children become confident self-researchers and to learn to trust their self-knowledge.

Many children say that their brain worked well because they were *happy* and that it didn't work well because they were *sad* and *unhappy.*
While these are very good reasons, help children find others, prompting if necessary:
     'You were *happy*, so maybe your brain was… *relaxed?'*
     'You were *sad*, so maybe you were worried about something and your brain was… *tense?'*, etc.

Ask them to write, using Activity 5 sheets,
why in **their opinion** their brains worked well
or
why in **their opinion** their brains went on strike.

Emphasise that everybody is different and that there are no right or wrong answers here.

•   ALL TRUE ANSWERS ARE CORRECT

Remember a situation when your brain seemed to have gone on strike and didn't want to work.
Why do you think that was?
Complete the sentences below.

My brain didn't want to work when ....

....

My brain went on strike because ....

....

Now remember a situation when your brain was working really well.
Why do you think it worked well then?
Complete the sentences below.

My brain was working well when ....

....

My brain was working well because ....

....

Activity 6

Some activities in this book are designed to help children understand the meaning of the brain's hemispheric dominance. This knowledge may help children select the most suitable learning strategies; at the same time it gives you a chance to have a closer look at their individual preferences.

Talk to children about the two hemispheres, draw pictures on the white board. You may want to copy this page and give it to each child, depending on how deep you want to go into the theory of hemispheric dominance. The decision to share it with the children or not is yours - you know your children and you will know what to share.

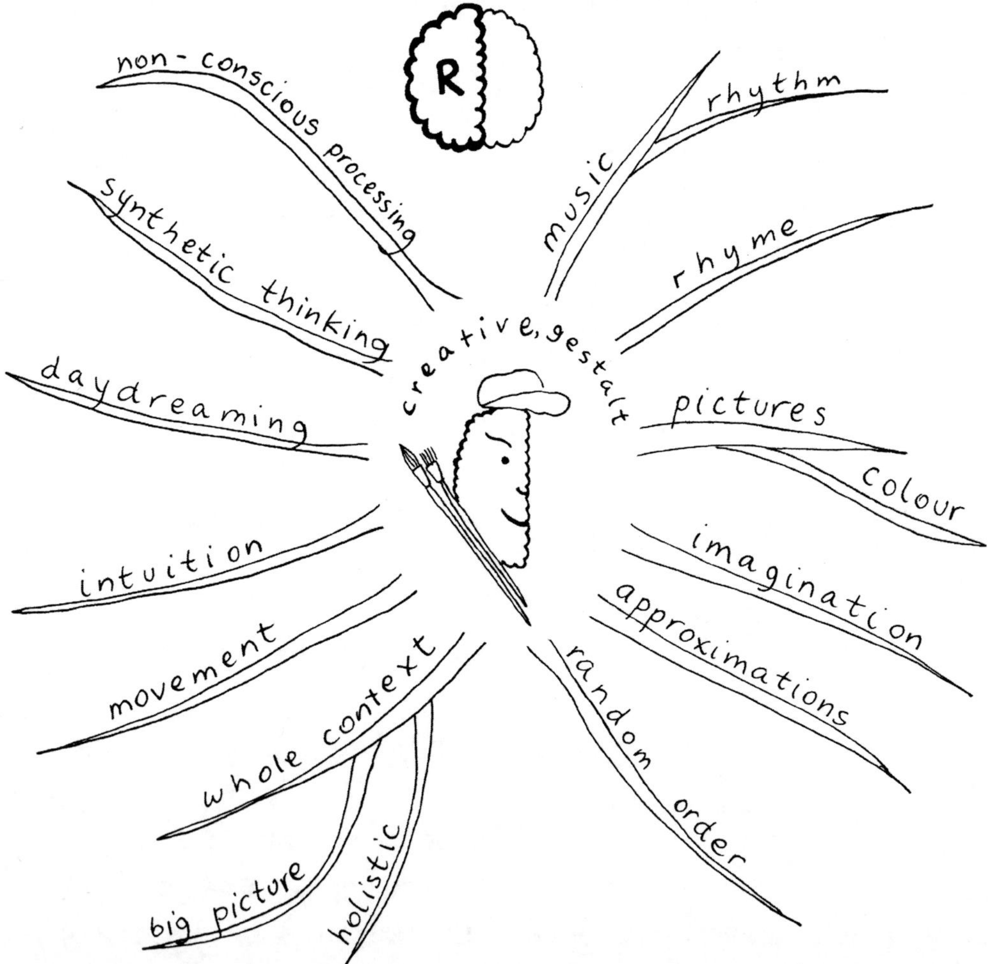

R

- non-conscious processing
- synthetic thinking
- daydreaming
- intuition
- movement
- whole context
- big picture
- holistic
- random order
- approximations
- imagination
- colour
- pictures
- rhyme
- music
- rhythm

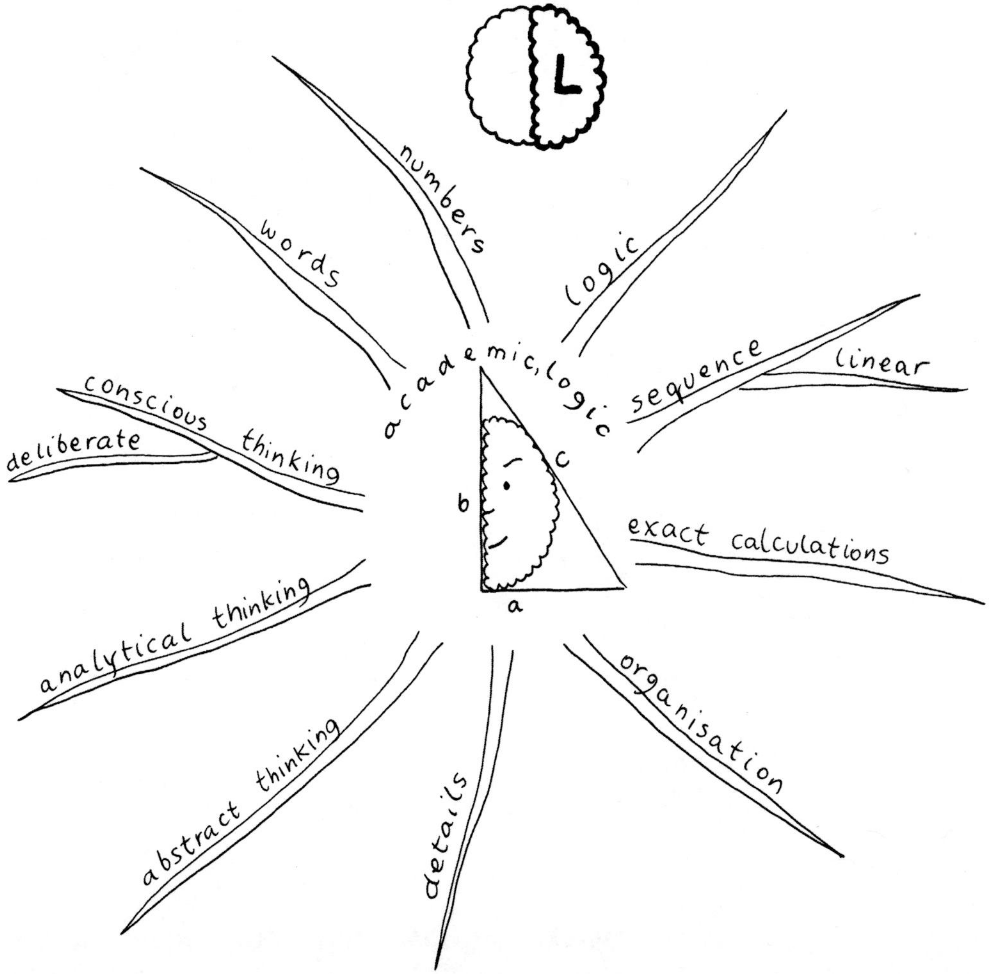

creative, gestalt

L

- numbers
- words
- logic
- linear
- sequence
- exact calculations
- organisation
- abstract thinking
- details
- analytical thinking
- deliberate
- conscious thinking

academic, logic

a b c

On the lines coming out of the brain picture, write the most important functions of your right and left hemispheres.
Remember, when you look at the smiling brain, its right side is on your left. If you need help, ask your friend or your teacher.

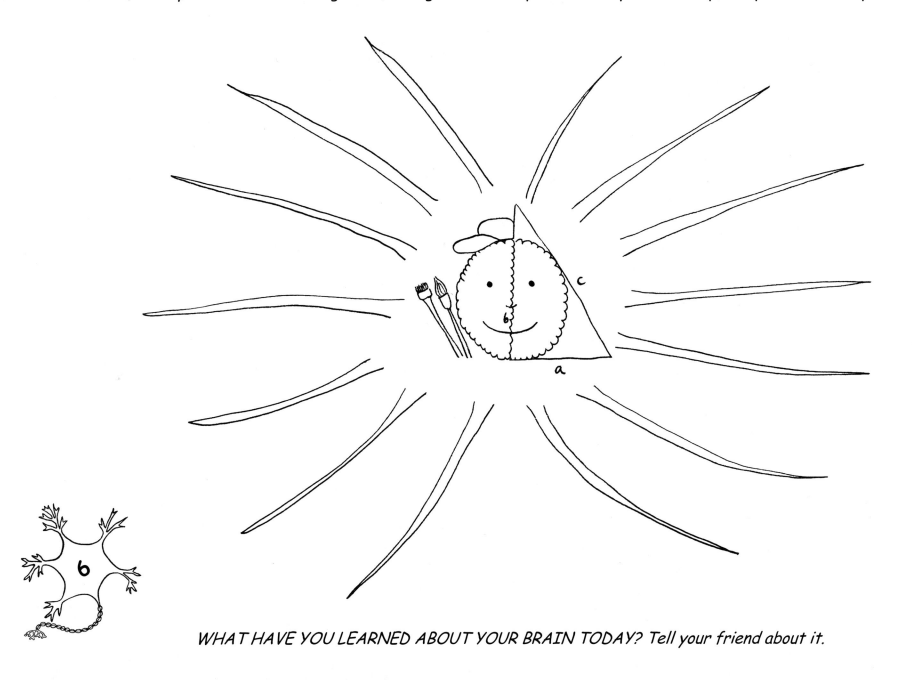

WHAT HAVE YOU LEARNED ABOUT YOUR BRAIN TODAY? Tell your friend about it.

Teacher's notes

When attempting to look at the hemispheric dominance, it is necessary to remember that **everybody has two working hemispheres. The brain's ideal state is full integration, i.e. having access to all Right (Gestalt) and Left (Logic) functions** (see Introduction). However, under pressure we tend to get locked in our dominant hemisphere, which makes whole-brain functioning difficult, sometimes even impossible.

Our response to stress is a pretty reliable way of determining our hemispheric dominance. This is when most people display predominantly 'right' or 'left brain' characteristics.

Carla Hannaford* maintains that under stress and when learning new things people who get locked in their **Left (Logic)** hemisphere

- **have poorer than usual comprehension**
- **do poorer work than usual**
- **'get on' with their work despite feeling tense**
- **give the impression of being insensitive, mechanical and tense.**

People who get locked in their **Right (Gestalt)** hemisphere tend to

- **forget the details**
- **be unable to think**
- **be unable to hear what people say**
- **be unable to understand what they are reading**
- **give the impression of being overwhelmed, emotional and 'spaced-out'.**

For some, this state may last for a few seconds only and most people need just a few minutes to get back to normal and re-connect two sides of the brain. However, some right-brain dominant learners may need a much longer time to regain the integrated state. A drink of water, a couple of deep breaths and a Cook's Hook-up can be extremely beneficial (see Activity 8).

Emphasise that everybody is different and that there are no right or wrong answers here.

- ALL TRUE ANSWERS ARE CORRECT

Think about a situation when you were learning something but were very stressed, worried and nervous.
Circle what it was like for you.

A 1.   You managed to remember
what you had learned.

2.   It was not easy to think but you somehow managed
to concentrate on your work.

3.   You felt tense but
your brain was working.

YES!
THAT'S ME!

4.   Your breathing was shallow and your heart was
beating fast but you could still think.

5.   You immediately got down to work.

Or for a moment (sometimes a little longer).

B 1.   You couldn't remember anything you had learned, your mind went blank.

2.   You felt your brain had gone on strike.

3.   You couldn't concentrate on your work.

4.   You couldn't hear what people where saying to you.

5.   You found it impossible to think clearly.

Whichever it is, THE MOST IMPORTANT THING IS TO RE-CONNECT YOUR BRAIN HEMISPHERES.
You will soon learn how to do this.

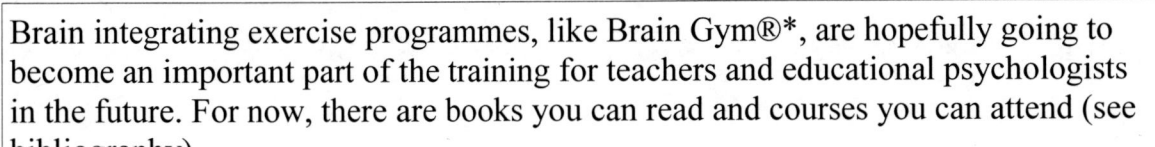

Brain integrating exercise programmes, like Brain Gym®*, are hopefully going to become an important part of the training for teachers and educational psychologists in the future. For now, there are books you can read and courses you can attend (see bibliography).

In Activity 8a and 8b you will find examples of some of Dennison's Brain Gym® exercises.

HOOK-UPs

close the electrical circuit in the body, containing and thus focusing disorganised energy. They have a soothing effect on our nervous system; freely circulating energy relaxes our mind and body.

Here is a quick way to relax and be able to think again:

1. **Have a drink of water (tap or bottled still).**

2. **Stand up or sit up straight, take a deep breath and slowly breathe all the air out.**

3. **Do a Cook's Hook-up.**

Breathe in… and out… in… and out…

BRAIN BUTTONS

By pressing and massaging the small indentations under the collarbone, we stimulate the carotid arteries that supply freshly oxygenated blood to the brain. This, in turn, improves our vision and attention.

Tell the children: *No matter how you react to pressure, you will think and learn much better when you learn how to relax and re-connect the two halves of your brain.*

TOO MUCH STRESS CLOSES OUR LEARNING CHANNELS!

Colour in the pictures or draw your own which will remind you what to do when you need your brain to work well.

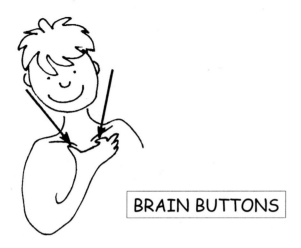

BRAIN BUTTONS

With the thumb and the middle finger, find two small dents below your collarbones (near the place where your collarbones meet your breast bone).

Massage your Brain Buttons every time you feel tired and find it difficult to think.

COOK'S HOOK-UP

Stand straight and breathe...
Stretch your arms in front of you,
back of hands together, thumbs pointing down.
Cross one hand over the other so palms are facing.
Interlock fingers and thumbs.
Turn twist inwards till you reach position in the picture.
Cross your legs and breathe...

H_2O
(still!)

slowly in....
....slowly out...

in...
out...

out...
in...

1   2   3

BUTTERFLY'S WINGS (Dennison's 'Lazy 8s')

Drawing the sign of infinity enables the child to cross the visual body midline and activates both eyes, integrating the right and left visual fields.

CROSS PAT AND CROSS WALK (Dennison's 'Cross Crawl')

Cross Crawl stimulates the brain for crossing the visual-auditory-kinaesthetic-tactile midline, for left-to-right eye movements and for improved both-eye vision. It activates both hemispheres of the brain, making learning easier.

Tell the children: *No matter how you react to pressure, you will think and learn much better when you learn how to relax and re-connect the two halves of your brain.*

TOO MUCH STRESS CLOSES OUR LEARNING CHANNELS!

Colour in the pictures or draw your own which will remind you what to do when you need your brain to work well.

BUTTERFLY'S WINGS

Put your hands in front of you and interlock the fingers.

Start drawing the wings of a butterfly in the air:
begin in the middle where the lines cross,
go up to the right and down, through the middle,
up to the left and down, through the middle,
up to the right and down, through the middle,
up to the left and down, and so on.
Keep your eyes focused on the thumbs.

Now make a fist with your right hand and,
keeping your eyes on the sticking out thumb,
draw *BUTTERFLY'S WINGS* in the air.
Change hands and do the same with your left hand.
And now both hands together…
Your head stays in one place, only your eyes and arms move!

Sit on a chair.

Lift your *right knee* and pat it with your *left hand.*

Lift your *left knee* and pat it with your *right hand.*

Repeat slowly ten times.

CROSS PAT and CROSS WALK

Stand up.

Lift your *right knee* and touch it with your *left elbow.*

Lift your *left knee* and touch it with your *right elbow.*

Repeat slowly ten times.

REMEMBER TO BREATHE AND DRINK WATER WHEN YOU DO THE EXERCISES.

Activity 9a

Teacher's notes

Activities 9a, 9b, and 9c constitute one whole exercise.

Please make sure that children know that it is perfectly OK to circle all the questions, to circle a few or none at all.

In activity 9a children are asked to mark which of the **left-brain** functions and behaviours they identify with.

Remind the children that

all the activities are part of an exciting and enjoyable exploration of our wonderfully diverse minds.

Read the questions and circle those to which your answer is YES.

If your answer is 'SOMETIMES' put a tick next to the question.

You may circle all the questions or none at all. Whatever you mark, you are right!

1. Do you have a good
   sense of time?
   (Can you tell when 1 hour has gone?)

2. Do you really like
   step-by-step instructions?

3. Do you always want
   to use a ruler when
   drawing lines?

4. Would you say that you are
   a well organised person?
   (Are your drawers tidy? Do you
   remember what to do and when?)

5. Do you prefer
   reading words
   to looking at pictures?

6. Do you notice small things
   before you see the whole picture?
   (Do you see the pattern on the material
   first, then the whole dress?)

7. Do you enjoy word games?

8. Do you like planning
   and making lists of
   things to do ?

9. Do you prefer black and white
   sketches to colour pictures?

10. Are you happy to follow rules
    which tell you what to do
    and how to do it?

WHAT HAVE YOU LEARNED ABOUT YOURSELF TODAY?

Activity 9b

Teacher's notes

Activities 9a, 9b, and 9c constitute one whole exercise.

Please make sure that children know that it is perfectly OK to circle all the questions, to circle a few or none at all.

In activity 9b children are asked to mark which of the **right-brain** functions and behaviours they identify with.

Remind the children that

all the activities are part of an exciting and enjoyable exploration of our wonderfully diverse minds.

Read the questions and circle those to which your answer is YES.
If your answer is 'SOMETIMES' put a tick next to the question.
You may circle all the questions or none at all. Whatever you mark, you are right!,

1. Do you learn the tune of a song before you learn the words?

2. Can you easily imagine pictures in your head?

3. Are colours important to you? (e.g. Do you prefer colour sheets to plain white?)

4. Do you prefer looking at pictures to reading words ?

5. Do you sometimes have fantastic ideas in your head?

6. Do you like to be in cosy looking rooms?

7. Do you enjoy sports? Do you like dancing?

8. Do you enjoy daydreaming a lot?

9. Do you want to know the end of the story before you finish reading it?

10. Do you see pictures in your head when you think?

WHAT HAVE YOU LEARNED ABOUT YOURSELF TODAY? Tell your friend about it.

Activity 9c

Teacher's notes

This activity combines Activities 9a and 9b and may make it clearer whether a child tends to function from a particular hemisphere.

Children who may have a tendency to function more often from their RIGHT brain will probably circle most of the following:

1, 4, 5, 7, 8, 10, 13, 14, 17, 18.

Children who may have a tendency to function more often from their LEFT brain will probably circle most of the following:

2, 3, 6, 9, 11, 12, 15, 16, 19, 20.

If the difference between the numbers of right and left brain circles is significant, it will reveal a child's learning needs and learning preferences.
If the difference is not significant, **the learning strategies selected by the child** will be an important indicator of his or her dominant tendencies.

Choices made earlier in Activity 1:
1, 3, 6, 8, 9, 11 may also suggest Right (Gestalt) brain preferences;
2, 4, 5, 7, 10, 12 may also suggest Left (Logic) brain tendencies.

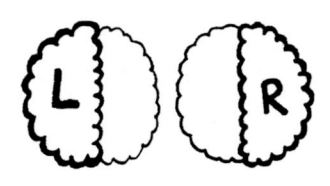

Photocopy this activity on colour sheets.

Tell the children that they may recognise some questions from previous questionnaires but tell them that because sometimes we may feel differently about things, the answers they give today might be different from the answers they have given previously.

Remind the children that it is neither good nor bad to be the way they are.

- EVERYBODY IS DIFFERENT
- PEOPLE LIKE DIFFERENT THINGS
- ALL TRUE ANSWERS THEY GIVE ARE THE RIGHT ANSWERS

Circle all the questions to which your answer is YES.

1. Do you enjoy daydreaming?

2. Do you have a good sense of time?

3. Do you really like following step-by-step instructions?

4. Do you want to know the end of the story before you finish reading it?

5. Do you see pictures in your head when you think?

6. Do you prefer black and white sketches to coloured pictures?

7. Do you enjoy dancing or sports?

8. Do you like cosy looking rooms?

9. Do you like using rulers to draw lines?

10. Do you sometimes have fantastic ideas in your head?

11. Do you think you are a well organised person?

12. Do you follow the rules which tell you how to do things (most of the time...) ?

13. Do you prefer pictures to words?

14. Are colours important to you?

15. Do you prefer words to pictures?

16. Do you notice small things (details) first before you see the whole thing?

17. Can you imagine things easily in your head?

18. Do you learn the tune before you learn the words of a song?

19. Do you enjoy playing word games?

20. Do you like planning your days and making lists of things to do?

9^c

YES!
THAT'S ME!

WHAT HAVE YOU LEARNED ABOUT YOURSELF TODAY?

Activity 10

Here is a list of strategies which *learners with left-brain tendencies* may find easy and useful:

- **putting information in a sequential order**
- **concentrating on details (looking at or thinking about small parts of the subject first)**
- **talking about the new subject (telling someone, or recording the new information)**
- **writing about the new subject**
- **teaching a friend by giving him/her step-by-step instructions of what to do**
- **finding logic in the subject, thinking about cause and effect.**

It may be a good idea to:
- **use mind-mapping to see the big picture, to see how details are connected**
- **do brain integration exercises to re-connect different parts of the brain.**

All learning strategies need to be fully understood by children, if they are to play a significant part in their learning. Explain the strategies and give examples wherever possible, so that children really understand them well.

Ask children to mark (in different colours)
everything they **already do** when they learn,
things which they **might enjoy doing**, which feel right for them,
and select one thing which is NOT their favourite but which **may help** them learn.

Ask the children to write in the clouds their **favourite learning strategies**.

Ask the children:

WHAT HAVE YOU LEARNED ABOUT YOURSELF TODAY?

Here is a list of learning tips which people with a certain kind of brain 'wiring' may find useful.
Mark anything that in your opinion could help you learn.

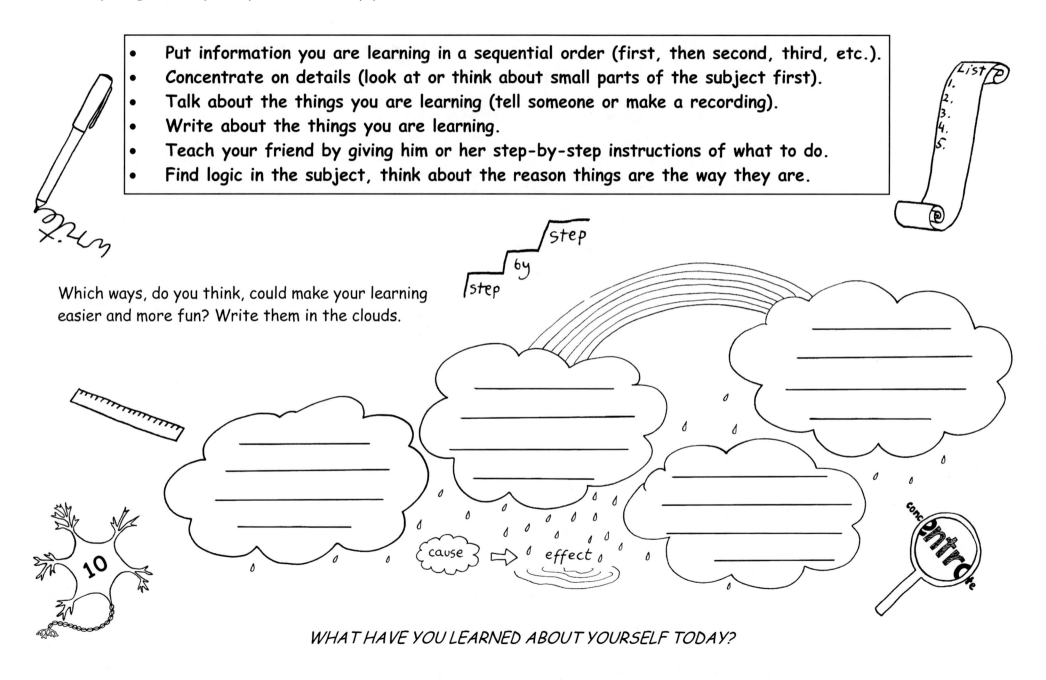

- Put information you are learning in a sequential order (first, then second, third, etc.).
- Concentrate on details (look at or think about small parts of the subject first).
- Talk about the things you are learning (tell someone or make a recording).
- Write about the things you are learning.
- Teach your friend by giving him or her step-by-step instructions of what to do.
- Find logic in the subject, think about the reason things are the way they are.

Which ways, do you think, could make your learning easier and more fun? Write them in the clouds.

step
by
step

cause ➪ effect

10

WHAT HAVE YOU LEARNED ABOUT YOURSELF TODAY?

Activity 11

Teacher's notes

Here is a list of strategies which ***learners with right-brain tendencies*** may find easy and useful:

- **learning and moving at the same time - acting out what you are learning, writing in big letters (a kinaesthetic activity in itself), squeezing a rubber ball, twisting pipe cleaners**
- **seeing the whole topic first before learning the details (e.g. the contents of a textbook)**
- **having some quiet time alone when learning something new and when under stress**
- **using stories, metaphors and examples that illustrate the subject**
- **finding a pleasant and cosy place to work**
- **being as relaxed as possible so you can think without any pressure**
- **using colour highlighters.**

It may be a good idea to:
- **use mind-mapping to see what role details play in the 'big picture'**
- **do brain integration exercises to re-connect different parts of the brain.**

All learning strategies need to be fully understood by children, if they are to play a significant part in their learning. Explain the strategies and give examples wherever possible, so that children really understand them well.

Ask children to mark (in different colours)
everything they **already do** when they learn,
things which they **might enjoy doing**, which feel right for them,
and select one thing which is NOT their favourite but which **may help** them learn.

Ask the children to write in the clouds their **favourite learning strategies**.

Ask the children:

WHAT HAVE YOU LEARNED ABOUT YOURSELF TODAY?

Here is a list of learning tips which people with a certain kind of brain 'wiring' may find useful.
Mark anything that in your opinion could help you learn.

- Learn and move at the same time (act out what you are learning, write in big letters, squeeze a rubber ball, twist pipe cleaners).
- See the whole topic first before you learn the details (the contents page of your book?).
- Have some quiet time alone when learning new things and when you feel nervous.
- Make up stories, use metaphors and examples that illustrate what you are learning.
- Have a pleasant and cosy place to do your work.
- Try to be as relaxed as possible so that you can think without any pressure.
- Use colour highlighters to mark important things.

Which ways, do you think, could make your learning easier and more fun? Write them in the clouds.

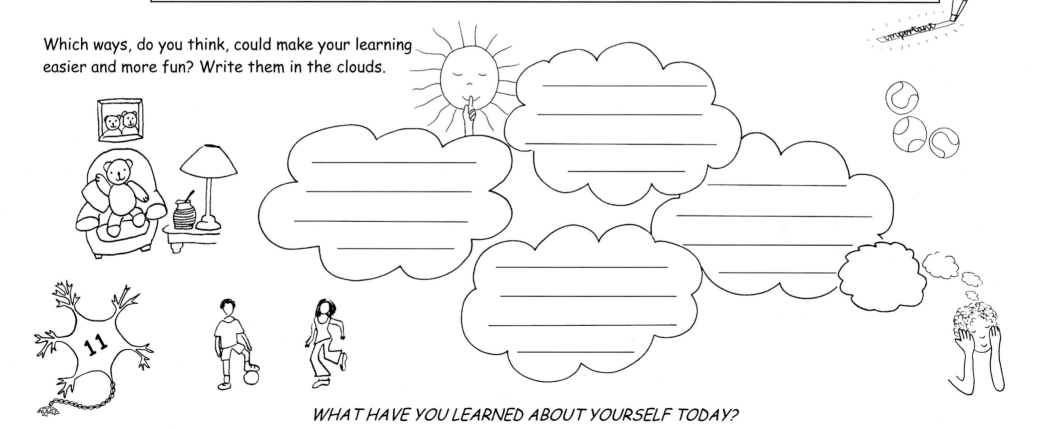

WHAT HAVE YOU LEARNED ABOUT YOURSELF TODAY?

Ask children to remind themselves what THEIR brains need to work well.

MOST

relaxed environment

movement

LEARNERS

challenge

'big picture' (whole context)

colours

THRIVE

chaNGE ON:

humour

music

integrated state = 'switched on' (Brain Gym®)

oxygen

ALL

good 'brain food'

water

NEED:

interest!

Ask children to write on the lines as neatly as they can and to draw pictures to illustrate their notes using colouring pens.

Children who want to write more can add more branches.

Then laminate each sheet and tell children to keep them on their tables as constant reminders.

It is important, however, to **USE** THE SELECTED STRATEGIES and to **try out** new ones, at times dropping some of the others.

You know better now what to do, when you want to learn something. On each line coming out of the picture of the happy brain write/draw one things you know YOUR brain likes and which will make your learning better and more fun. Add lines, if you need more.

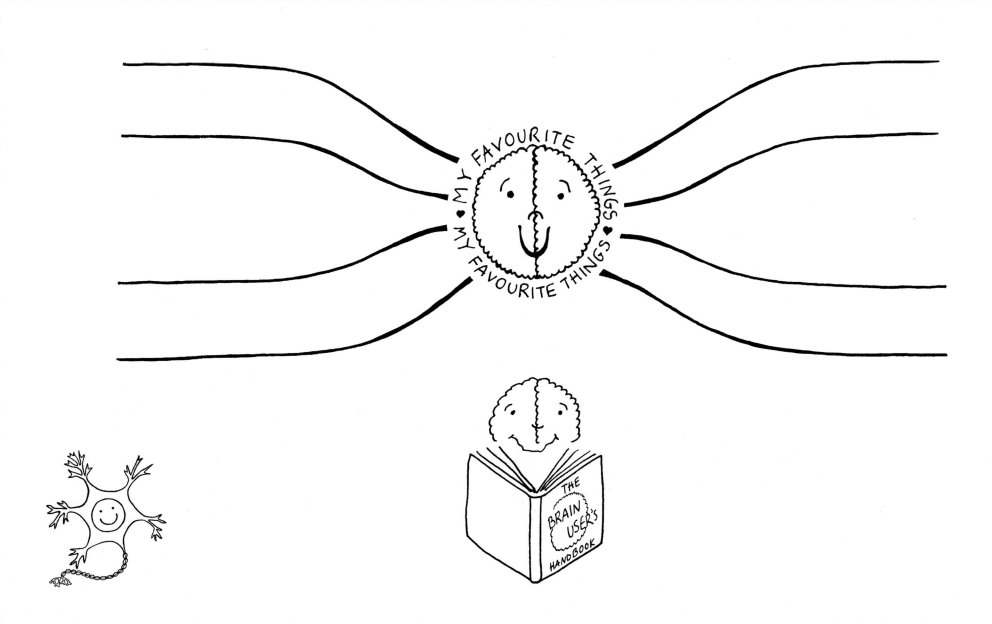

A few books you may find interesting:

Buzan, Tony. *HEAD FIRST*. Harper Collins, 2000
Claxton, Guy. *HARE BRAIN TORTOISE MIND*. Fourth Estate, 1998
De Porter, Bobbi and Hernacki, Mike. *QUANTUM LEARNING*. Piatkus, 1993
Gardner, Howard. *INTELLIGENCE REFRAMED*. Basic Books, 1999
Hannaford, Carla. *THE DOMINANCE FACTOR*. Great Ocean Publishers, 1997
Hannaford, Carla. *AWAKENING THE CHILD HEART*. Jamilla Nur Publishing, 2002
Hoffman, Eva & Bartkowicz, Z. *THE LEARNING ADVENTURE*. Learn To Learn, 1999
Hoffman, Eva. *A GUIDE TO THE LEARNING ADVENTURE*. Learn To Learn, 1999
Hughes, Mike. *CLOSING THE LEARNING GAP*. Network Educational Press, 1999
Jansen, Eric. *BRAIN COMPATIBLE STRATEGIES*. The Brain Store, Inc., 1997
Jansen, Eric. *TEACHING WITH THE BRAIN IN MIND*. ASCD, 1998
Krebs, Charles. *A REVOLUTIONARY WAY OF THINKING*. Hill of Content, 1998
Robertson, Ian. *MIND SCULPTURE*. Bantam Press, 1999
Smith, Alistair. *THE BRAIN'S BEHIND IT*. Network Educational Press, 2002
Smith, Alistair and Call, Nicola. *THE ALPS APPROACH*. Network Educational Press, 1999
Vos, Jeanette and Dryden, Gordon. *THE LEARNING REVOLUTION*. The Learning Web, rev. 1997

Brain integration courses:

Educational Kinesiology Foundation - London, UK
L.E.A.P. (Learning Enhancement Advanced Program) - Learning Enhancement Centre, Boulder, Colorado, USA

For more information about this work as well as about the whole range of our activities, please contact us:

tel: +44 (0)1458 830641 / +44 (0)7976 892976
learntolearn@connectfree.co.uk
www.inspiredlearning.info

We run workshops for
- teachers who wish to experience guiding children towards the fascinating discovery of their learning profiles
- teachers who already work this way but want to acquire better skills and gain more confidence in their work
- teachers and children, giving practical demonstrations of the way this work can be done
- parents wishing to expand their guiding skills in helping their children learn better